My First Montessori Book of Patterns

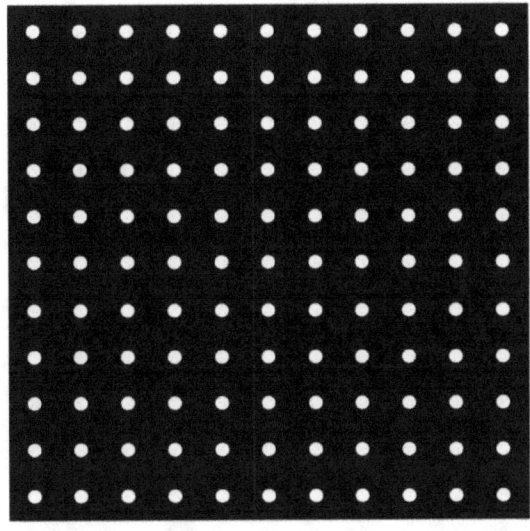

MARY DA PRATO

Illustrated By

MARY DA PRATO
and
GENEVIEVE DeVANEY DA PRATO

ISBN: 1492974803
ISBN-13: 978-1492974802

DISCLAIMERS

Select information presented in *My First Montessori Book of Patterns* is based upon Montessori principles as presented to the author through her AMI Primary Montessori training. Many of the suggested activities in the "For Parents" section of this publication, while based upon Montessori educational philosophy and techniques, are not necessarily official Montessori presentations. While "Patterns" is not an official presentation in the Montessori Casa, they can be introduced using Montessori techniques to enhance and expand the child's knowledge following initial "Fabric Box" presentations.

In this publication, students are called "he" and guides are called "she." This designation, assigned for the reader's convenience, in no way reflects the gender dynamic of teachers and students in a Montessori environment.

argyle

basket weave

bull's-eye

calico

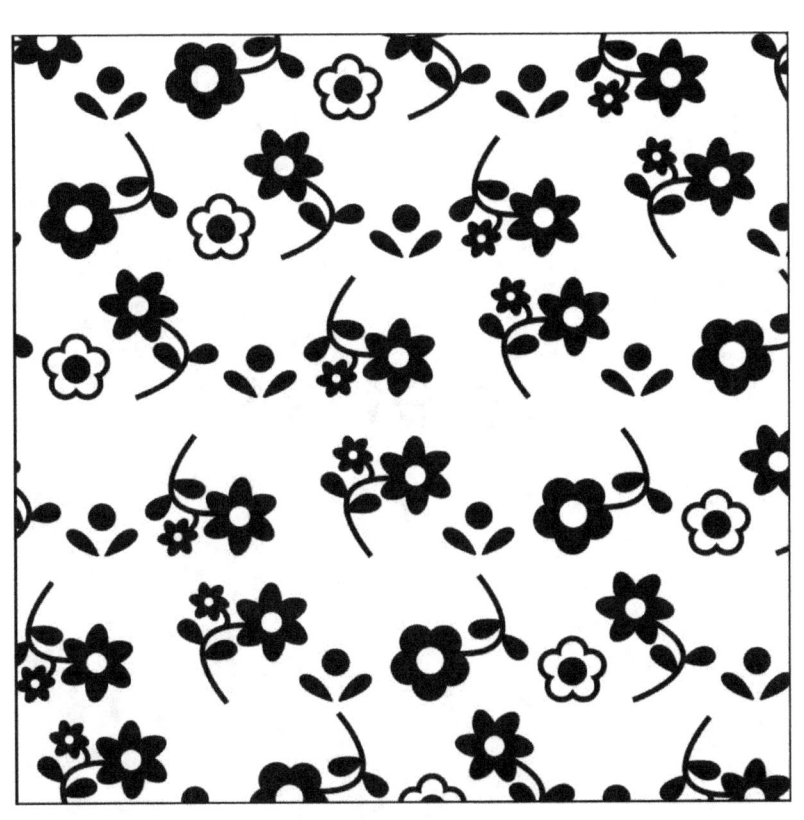

checks

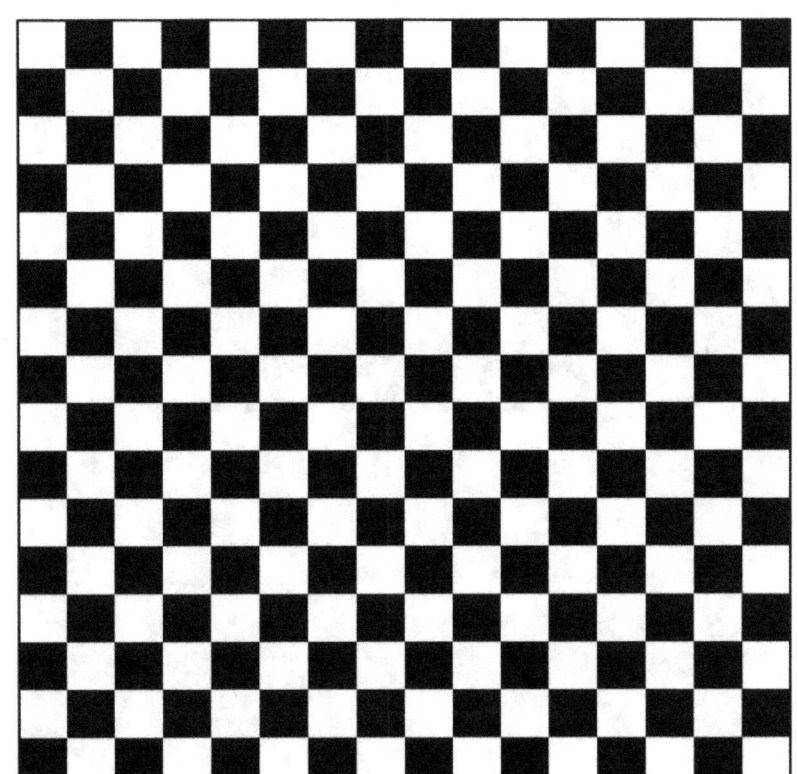

chevron

egg and dart

fish scale

floral

graph check

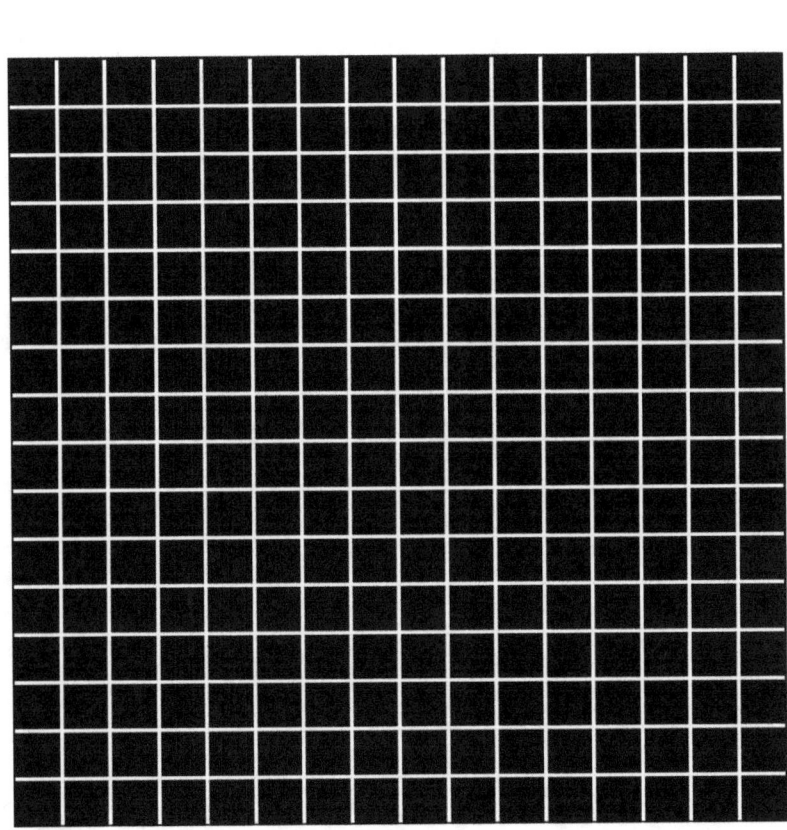

Greek key

herringbone

honeycomb

hound's-tooth

lattice

ogee

paisley

pinstripes

plaid

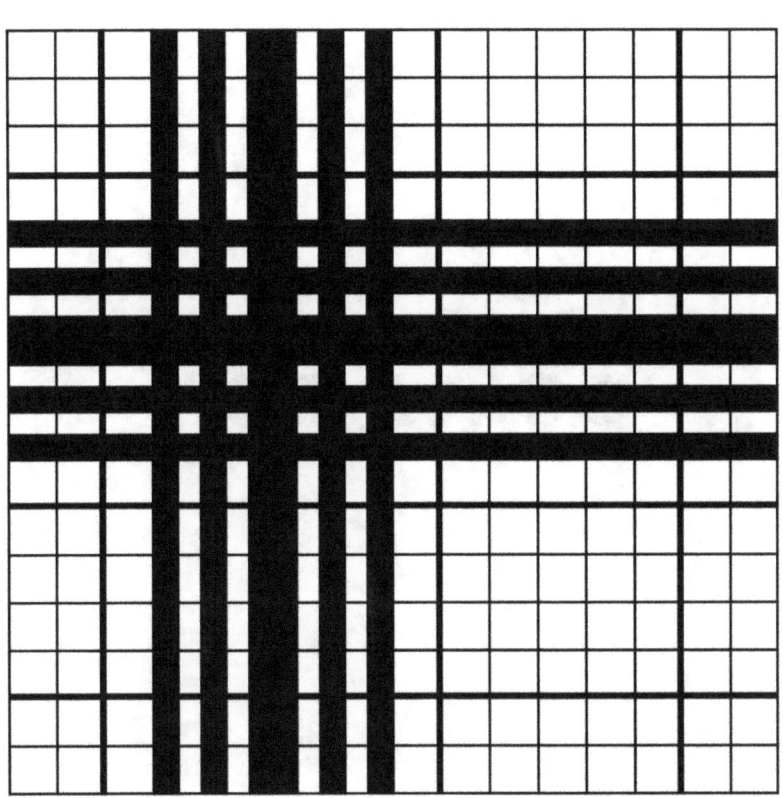

polka dots

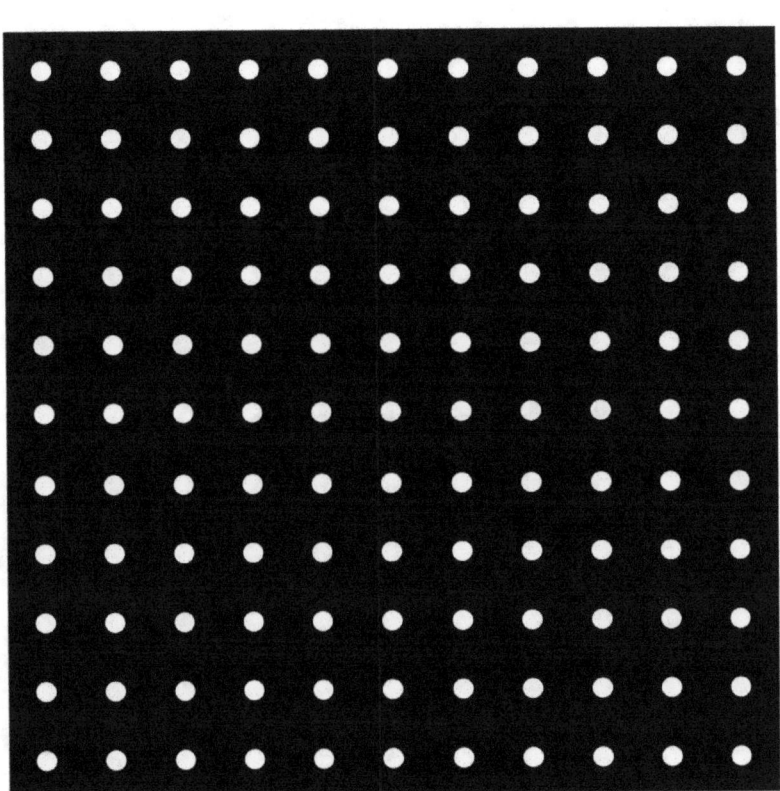

quatrefoil

scroll

serpentine

stripes

vermicular

FOR PARENTS

Illustrations in *My First Montessori Book of Patterns* are inspired by the hands-on "Fabric Boxes" exercises in the Sensorial section of the Casa, or classroom for three through six year old children. Sensorial materials are designed to strengthen and refine the five senses of touch, vision, hearing, smell, and taste as well as their qualities. "Qualities" are the perceptible aspects of a particular sense. There are three qualities for the sense of touch, or three perceptions that can be felt by humans: thermic, texture, and baric. Two Fabric Boxes, initially introduced to children approximately three-and-a-half years of age at a purely sensorial level in the prepared environment, help refine a child's perception of texture. The Fabric Boxes and their related activities serve the following purposes:

- Awareness of texture is developed.
- Tactile perception is refined.
- Names of various natural fabrics in "Fabric Box 1" are introduced and reinforced.
- Specialty fabric weaves in "Fabric Box 2" are introduced and reinforced.
- Fabrics in the Fabric Boxes provide a catalyst for history and geography studies related to how, when, and where fabrics originated.
- A variety of fabric weaves are compared and discussed following hands-on experience.

In the Montessori Casa, or classroom for three to six year old children, students refine their tactile perception, or sense of texture, by pairing fabrics from two Fabric Box sets. "Pairing" is when a child pairs or matches Sensorial materials based upon the quality presented.

Thermic Bottles

Pairing Thermic Bottles

The first Sensorial pairing experience in the Casa is "Thermic Bottles," an activity in which two sets of bottles containing hot, warm, cool, and cold water are matched to help the student refine the thermic quality of touch. For student safety, empty bottles are stored in their box on the shelf. The guide or her assistant fills the Thermic Bottles for the child prior to each use.

Following experience pairing Thermic Bottles, a child learns how to pair identically sized matching Fabric Box swatches by texture. A blindfold is worn when pairing fabrics so there are no visual hints. For hygiene, a disposable tissue is placed between the child's eyes and the blindfold to create a barrier. In some Casas, each child may have his own blindfold. Regardless of whether children use a tissue or a personal blindfold, all blindfolds in the Casa should be washed frequently for cleanliness.

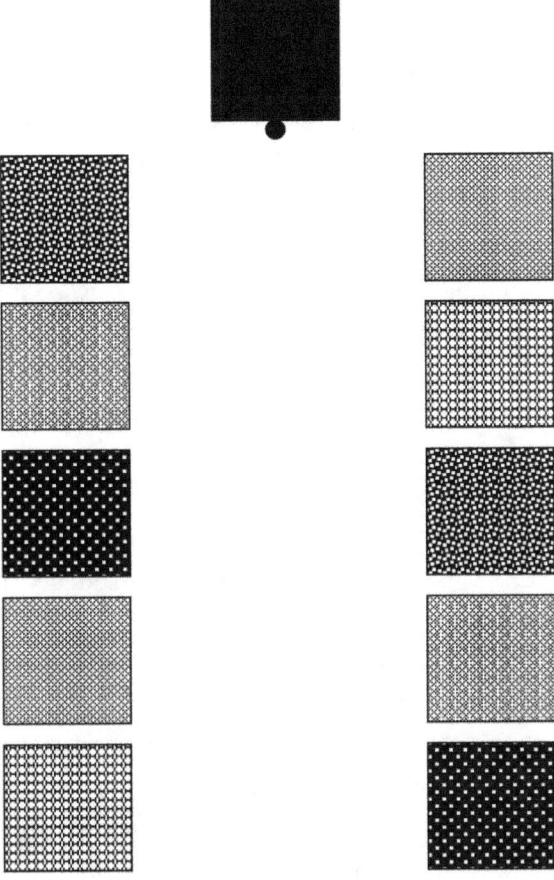

The first fabric box presented, called "Fabric Box 1," contains five or six pairs of identically sized fabric swatches approximately 4" x 4" or 4" x 5" in a variety of natural materials with contrasting textures such as wool, silk, cotton, linen, burlap, and denim. Pairs of fabric swatches in Fabric Box 1 are occasionally rotated with new fabric types to maintain the child's interest, encourage use, and expand tactile experiences.

To begin the first Fabric Box presentation, the guide shows the child where to find Fabric Box 1 and has him take the box to a table. Once at the table, the guide places the box at the top center of the workspace. She then retrieves a blindfold and places it beside Fabric Box 1. If the blindfold is communal, the guide also retrieves a clean tissue for hygiene.

Before opening Fabric Box 1, the guide says, "We always wash our hands before using a Fabric Box." If the child asks why hand washing is necessary prior to using the box, the guide gives a simple honest explanation such as, "Our hands make natural oils which can change how fabric feels, so we need to wash the oils away before we work." Keep in mind that young children may accept hand washing as part of the presentation and not question its necessity. In this scenario, a verbal explanation may not be needed. The guide will know whether or not to provide commentary about hand washing based upon her observations of the individual child.

After the guide and child thoroughly wash their hands at the sink with soap and water, the guide may invite the child to sensitize his fingertips. Sensitizing fingertips, the act of submerging the fingertips in warm water and then scrubbing them dry with a clean terry cloth towel to temporarily increase their sensitivity, helps children feel minute differences between and among varying degrees of texture. While essential for other Sensorial activities related to texture, sensitizing the fingertips is optional when working with the Fabric Boxes.

Once the guide and child have washed their hands and possibly sensitized their fingertips, they return to their work table to continue the presentation. The blindfold is not used at this point.

The guide opens Fabric Box 1, which contains sets of swatches to match, and removes the first swatch. Without speaking, she holds the swatch between the palms of her hands in midair and rubs her hands together in order to feel the swatch between the entire surface area of her palms. After demonstrating how to feel the fabric swatch, the guide hands the swatch to the child and says, "Now it's your turn." The child should then imitate the guide, feeling the swatch between his palms. When he is finished, the guide takes the fabric swatch from the child and places it in the upper right-hand corner of the table below and slightly to the right of Fabric Box 1. (See "Fabric Box 1 Initial Layout.") After setting the swatch aside, the guide removes the next swatch from Fabric Box 1, feels it, gives the child a turn, and then places it under the first swatch with some space between the two swatches. The guide continues to remove swatches from Fabric Box 1, feel them, and place them in a column on the right-hand side of the table until the first set of fabric swatches in the box have been found. Once the five or six swatches have been located and arranged on the table, the guide brings the child's attention to the matching set of fabric swatches in the bottom of Fabric Box 1. For clarification, the guide says, "These fabric swatches are the same as the ones we just felt." The guide removes each swatch in Fabric Box 1 one at a time and lines them up vertically in random order on the left-hand side of the table across from the swatches lined up on the right-hand side of the table. As soon as the fabric swatches are arranged, the guide closes Fabric Box 1, puts on her blindfold, and says, "I am going to find the ones that match."

Fabric Box 1 Pairing in Progress

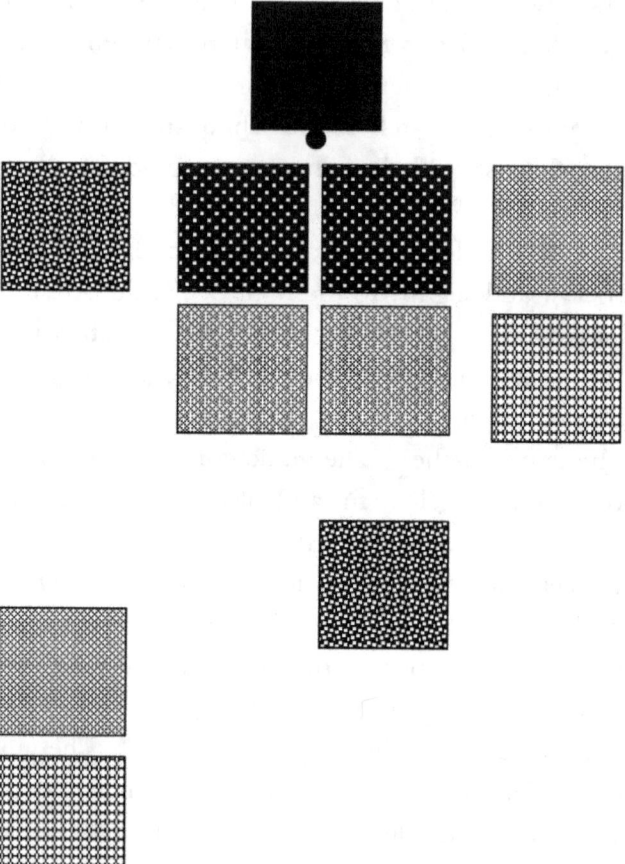

To pair or match fabric swatches systematically, the blindfolded guide picks up the fabric swatch closest to her on the right-hand side of the table and feels it between her palms as demonstrated earlier. She then places the swatch in front of her at the bottom of the table just slightly right of center. The guide then picks up the swatch closest to her on the left-hand side of the table and feels the second swatch between her palms to determine whether or not it matches the first swatch in front of her. If she is unsure, she can set the swatch down to the left of the first swatch and feel the first one again. If the swatches match, the guide slides them together side-by-side horizontally and pushes them vertically to the top of the table until they are directly below Fabric Box 1. The guide picks up the next swatch from the right-hand column, feels it between her palms, and places it in front of her at the bottom of the workspace slightly right of center. She now systematically searches by touch for the fabric swatch's match from the left-hand column. If the swatches do not match, the guide returns the fabric swatch from the left-hand column to its original position and picks up the swatch immediately above it. She feels the swatch from the left-hand column between her palms to determine if it matches the swatch from the right-hand column. Once again, she can always set the second swatch down and feel the first to confirm a match. The blindfolded guide continues to pair fabric swatches in this manner until all swatches are lined up vertically in pairs in the middle of the table from top to bottom as illustrated in "Fabric Box 1 Final Layout."

Fabric Box 1 Final Layout

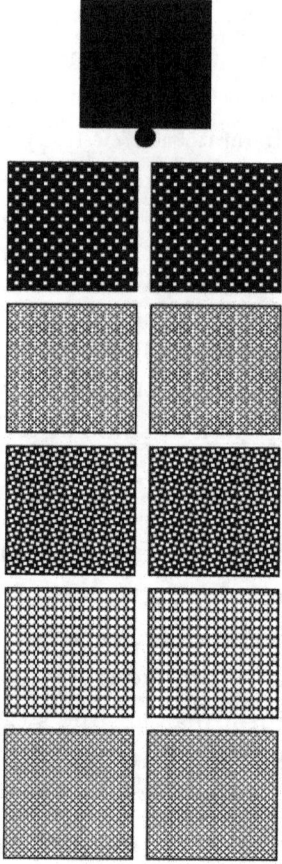

After pairing all fabric swatches, the guide removes her blindfold to see how many she matched correctly. The differences in fabric colors and patterns make accuracy immediately apparent. Since young children have greater tactile sensitivity than adults,[1] it is not uncommon for a teacher to pair similar fabrics such as linen and hemp incorrectly. If this happens, the guide demonstrates friendliness toward error and smoothly transfers the activity to the student by saying, "Oh, it looks like I need more practice. But I will have to practice later because now it's your turn." The guide then helps the child rearrange the fabric swatches into columns on the right and left-hand sides of the table, making sure that swatches directly across from one another do not match. Once the materials are arranged in random order, the guide assists the child with his blindfold if necessary. She then retreats to observe and notes student progress in her records.

Following hands-on experience with the fabrics presented, the guide introduces three contrasting fabric names at a time such as "cotton," "wool," and "silk" in the form of a "Three Period Lesson." A Three Period Lesson is a game-like technique used in the Casa to introduce and reinforce new vocabulary. The first period of the Three Period Lesson is called "Naming." During this stage, the guide places the three fabric swatches horizontally with space between them at the center of the workspace. She points to each fabric swatch in turn and says, "This is 'cotton.' This is 'wool.' This is 'silk.'" This concludes "Naming," the first period of the Three Period Lesson.

The second period of the Three Period Lesson, known as "Recognition," is the game-like portion of the activity. During this stage, the guide gives the child commands involving the fabric swatches such as, "Pick up the 'cotton,'" "Point to the 'silk,'" or "Slide the 'wool' here." To reinforce tactile interaction with the fabric swatches, the guide may occasionally incorporate commands

---

[1] Montessori, Maria. *The Discovery of the Child*. Trans. Mary A. Johnstone. Chennai: Kalakshetra, 2006. Print. Pages 244-245.

such as, "Touch the 'silk'" or "Feel the 'wool.'" To make the game more challenging, the guide may also have the child close his eyes while she rearranges the fabric swatches. After the guide has rearranged the swatches, the child opens his eyes and the game continues with additional commands. If at any time the child misidentifies a swatch, the guide affirms his choice by saying something like, "This is 'silk.' Now show me 'cotton.'" The guide continues to give commands involving cotton, wool, and silk to practice "Recognition" until the child is confident or loses interest.

The third period of the Three Period Lesson is called "Remembering." During this period of the Three Period Lesson, the guide points to each fabric swatch one at a time and asks, "What is this?" If the child misidentifies any fabric, the guide simply says the fabric's correct name without criticism or further commentary.

Following successful identification of each of the three fabric swatches, the guide asks the child if he would like to learn three more. If the child is interested, the guide introduces the names of three more fabrics using the Three Period Lesson technique. If the child is not interested, the guide asks him what he would like to do next. Generally, no more than six new vocabulary words in a given activity are introduced per day to avoid overwhelming the child.

Just as important as the Three Period Lesson technique is its application. A child in the Casa is never forced to complete a Three Period Lesson. If a student becomes bored or frustrated with the vocabulary presented, the guide gracefully closes the lesson by saying, "Thank you for playing with me. We can look at this some other time." Forced inflexible lessons only lead to frustration and resistance to future instruction. Respect for a child's interests at a given time promotes a positive attitude toward learning as its own reward. Since children are naturally curious, he will either return to the lesson when ready or learn it through osmosis by observing classmates due to the power of the absorbent mind. Either way, if the guide is patient and consistent, the child should eventually learn the vocabulary. Keep in mind that learning new vocabulary may require several or even dozens of repetitions of the Three Period Lesson over time depending on the individual child.

Following fabric vocabulary lessons, the guide may also introduce history and geography lessons that focus on a familiar fabric. When discussing silk, for example, the guide may bring out the Puzzle Map of Asia to show its Chinese origin, read a simple non-fiction book about the life cycle of silkworms, or show photographs of the silk manufacturing process. When discussing cotton, simple botany lessons about the cotton plant and where it grows can be incorporated into the guide's presentation. Further fabric explorations may include lessons about patterns and their histories, identifying and differentiating plant versus animal based fabrics, and simple sewing projects which use the fabrics discussed. These related activities may be presented to an individual child or to small groups of children over the course of a few days or until interest wanes. Lessons should always be fact-based, non-biased, and non-political as preschoolers typically do not possess a reasoning mind.[2]

---

[2] Montessori, Maria. *The Secret of Childhood*. Trans. Barbara B. Carter. Chennai: Orient Longman, 2006. Print. Page 217.

Fabric Box 2 Initial Layout

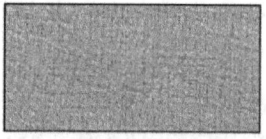

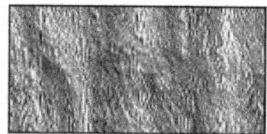

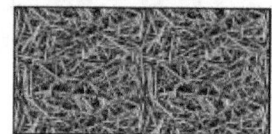

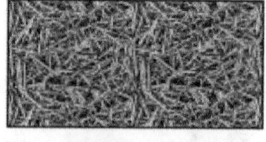

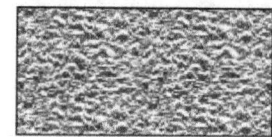

When a child exhausts the possibilities of Fabric Box 1, the guide introduces "Fabric Box 2." Fabric Box 2 contains five or six pairs of fabric swatches which showcase a variety of specialty weaves such as brocade, tapestry, silk charmeuse, corduroy, and tulle for a child's further tactile refinement. Since Fabric Box 2 is used in the same manner as Fabric Box 1, the guide's presentation with Fabric Box 2 is brief. She shows the child where to find Fabric Box 2 on the shelf and has him take it to a table. The guide also has the child retrieve a blindfold. Just as with Fabric Box 1, the guide has the child wash his hands and possibly sensitize his fingertips. When finished, they return to the table. The guide says, "We use this fabric box just like the other one." This is usually sufficient for the child to work independently. The guide retreats to observe and notes student progress in her records.

Fabric Box 2 Final Layout

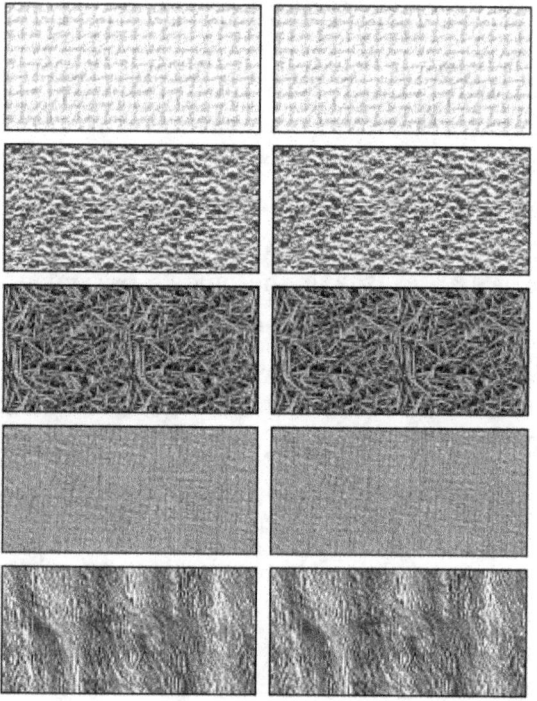

Following experience with Fabric Box 2, the guide may introduce the names of weaves three at a time in the form of a Three Period Lesson using the same technique as the Three Period Lesson for Fabric Box 1. Simple related history, geography, sewing, and pattern identification lessons may be introduced shortly thereafter.

You can make Fabric Boxes at home. Begin by finding two attractive child-sized boxes that are wide and deep enough to hold at least ten fabric swatches. It is strongly recommended that both boxes have a lid that is either hinged or rests atop the box. The boxes should look similar but not identical to provide a sense of order. Once you have found appropriate boxes for fabric storage, choose fabrics from your sewing remnants at home or take your child to the fabric store to select fabrics together. Since you will not require large amounts of fabric to make identical pairs of swatches, check the store's remnant pile first for inexpensive fabric pieces. Start by looking for fabrics to place in Fabric Box 1. Fabric Box 1, the first of the two Fabric Boxes introduced to children in the Casa, contains swatches of natural fabrics for pairing such as burlap, chiffon, cotton, denim, hemp, linen, rayon, satin, silk, taffeta, wool, and so forth. Look for examples of these and other fabrics at the store with your child. If you or your child find an unlabeled swatch, ask a store clerk to help you identify it. Fabric Box 1 should contain five or six pairs of unique fabrics. Fabric swatch pairs should be traded for new fabric pairs occasionally to maintain the child's interest. To allow for rotation, find or purchase at least ten different pairs of natural fabrics for the first box. Keep the extra swatches in a different location for later use. Remember to use or buy natural materials for this exercise instead of synthetics such as polyester and faux fur in accordance with the Montessori principle of providing children with real materials rather than synthetic substitutes. Rayon, a hybrid fabric, is appropriate for Fabric Box 1 as it is made from natural cellulose fibers.[3]

After you have gathered materials for Fabric Box 1, begin searching for swatches to place in Fabric Box 2. Fabric Box 2 focuses on specialty weaves such as brocade, corduroy, cotton batiste, damask, eyelet, jacquard, organdy, seersucker, silk charmeuse, tapestry, tulle, and so on. Follow the same fabric gathering procedure used for Fabric Box 1. Keep in mind that the main focus of Fabric Box 2 is to present the dramatic and subtle differences in weaves whereas Fabric Box 1 provides a more basic introduction to fabric textures. For this reason, Fabric Box 1 may contain some fine weaves such as taffeta as they do not distract from the original

[3] Cosgrove, John H. "Rayon." *World Book Online Reference Center.* World Book Encyclopedia. Web. 19 May 2013.

presentation.

Once you have assembled your materials for Fabric Box 1 and Fabric Box 2, cut your swatches with pinking shears. Use Fray Check™ to prevent raveling. Do not hem fabrics as this creates bulk which could be distracting to your child. While there are no official Fabric Box swatch measurements in the Casa, each fabric swatch should be large enough for your child to rub between his palms to sufficiently feel the fabric but not so large that it is overwhelming. Swatches may be square or rectangular. To help keep Fabric Box 1 and Fabric Box 2 swatches from becoming mixed up, you may want to choose different sizes of fabric swatches for each box.

In the Montessori Casa, experience precedes language. This means that a young child should have hands-on experience with a material before learning its accompanying vocabulary. Since children under the age of six or seven are concrete sensorial learners[4] who have not yet developed reason,[5] they learn best through hands-on experiences which engage one or more of the five senses. It is only after a child has had hands-on experience with a given material that related vocabulary can be effectively introduced, understood, and retained.[6] For this reason, make sure your child has had ample time to pair fabric swatches from your homemade Fabric Boxes with a blindfold before introducing any related vocabulary. If necessary, remind your child that the Fabric Box swatches are designed to be matched by touch rather than by sight. The child should close his eyes or wear a blindfold while pairing swatches. When finished, he should open his eyes or remove the blindfold to see how many he matched correctly. After randomly placing the fabric swatches into two columns, he should close his eyes or put his blindfold on before pairing swatches again.

---

[4] Montessori, Maria. *The Secret of Childhood.* Trans. Barbara B. Carter. Chennai: Orient Longman, 2006. Print. Page 153.

[5] Ibid. Page 217.

[6] Montessori, Maria. *Dr. Montessori's Own Handbook.* Mineola: Dover, 2005. Print. Pages 80-84.

Once your child has worked with the Fabric Boxes, you can introduce the names of contrasting fabrics three at a time in the form of a Three Period Lesson. During "Naming," the first period of the Three Period Lesson, point to each fabric in turn and say its name as in, "This is 'cotton,'" "This is 'wool,'" "This is 'silk.'" During the second period of the Three Period Lesson, give fun game-like commands for "Recognition" such as, "Feel the 'wool,'" "Hand me the 'silk,'" or "Put the 'cotton' here." To keep the game interesting and challenging, you can have your child close his eyes while you rearrange the three fabric swatches on the table. When your child opens his eyes, continue the game with additional commands until he is confident with the vocabulary or loses interest. To conclude the lesson, point to each fabric swatch in turn and ask, "What is this?" This is "Remembering," the third period of the Three Period Lesson. If at any time your child gives an incorrect answer, simply state the correct answer without commentary or criticism as in, "This is 'cotton.' Now show me 'silk.'" When your child correctly identifies the three fabric swatches, ask him if he would like to learn three more or if he would rather do something else. If your child is interested, put the three fabric swatches away and choose three more. Give the Three Period Lesson with the three new swatches. Introduce no more than six new fabric names per day to avoid overwhelming your child. Never force your child to complete a Three Period Lesson. If he becomes bored or frustrated during the lesson, gracefully end the activity by saying, "Thank you for playing with me. We can look at this some other time." After ending the lesson, supervise your child as he puts the swatches away and returns the Fabric Box to its proper place in its original condition. Help your child transition to the next activity. Return to the vocabulary lesson later in the day or the next day when your child demonstrates interest. Keep in mind that learning new vocabulary may require several or even dozens of repetitions of the Three Period Lesson over time depending on the individual child. Be patient.

After introducing fabric vocabulary, choose a fabric such as wool as a focal point for holistic lessons related to history and geography. It is important to plan your lessons carefully in order to give your child accurate, unbiased presentations about sheep, sheering wool, spinning yarn, dying yarn, weaving, and so on. Research the topic of "wool" independently before introducing any new information to your child. Choose credible sources for your initial research such as *World Book Encyclopedia* or *Encyclopedia Britannica.* Search for these encyclopedias and other reference books at your local library. Ask your local librarian if your library card allows you to access encyclopedias and other reference sources through their website from home. Also check out non-fiction books on your topic for further research. Prepare visual materials for your presentation.

When you have compiled your research and planned what you want to discuss, place the familiar wool swatch on a rug or table. Invite your child to sit with you. Make sure your child knows the vocabulary before you continue. To assess your child's readiness, say something like, "You have been doing a lot of work with Fabric Box 1 this week. You also learned some new fabric names." Pick up the wool swatch and show it to your child. Say, "What is this fabric called?" If your child correctly identifies the swatch as "wool," verbally reinforce his knowledge using a complete sentence such as, "Yes, this is 'wool.'" Begin your lesson about wool and where it comes from. A sample lesson about wool is explained in detail in the following paragraphs. If your child hesitates or does not remember the name of the fabric, say, "This is 'wool.'" Depending on your child's level of interest, you can gracefully end the lesson or say, "Let's find two more fabric swatches in Fabric Box 1!" Once you have chosen two more fabric swatches, initiate a Three Period Lesson with fabric names for review. When finished, thank your child for playing with you and help him transition to the next activity. Wait to present any related activities until your child is confident with the vocabulary. Flexibility and patience are crucial.

Once your child can accurately identify "wool" without

hesitation, begin your first related activity. Keep in mind that related activities are highly open-ended. How you present related activities will depend on your child's age, interests, abilities, and level of cognitive development. Regardless of your child's age, always speak in clear, complete, grammatically correct sentences to model proper language usage. Keep your presentation simple. Refrain from using superfluous words or presenting too much information at one time. Take the lead from your child. Be open to any commentary he provides spontaneously, but do not constantly question him as though you are conducting a test. Always be attentive to your child's level of interest. If he grows bored or frustrated with a lesson, gracefully end the activity by saying, "Thank you for playing with me. What would you like to do now?" Following is an open-ended example of how you may want to present activities related to wool to your child.

Show your child the wool swatch he has correctly identified. Say, "Yes, this is wool. Where does wool come from?" If your child treats your question as though it is rhetorical, continue your presentation. If he says, "Wool comes from sheep," you can say, "Yes, wool comes from sheep. We are going to talk about how wool comes from sheep." If your child gives an incorrect answer, such as, "Wool comes from the carpet," respond with a gentle correction such as, "Actually, our carpet is *made* of wool. Let me show you where wool comes from." Bring out the first visual aid that you have prepared for your lesson. In this case, your visual aid would probably be a photograph of a sheep. Show the picture to your child and ask, "What do you see here?" Once your child identifies the picture, you can ask, "What can you tell me about sheep?" Listen to your child's response to gage how to proceed. If your child already knows a lot about sheep including how their wool is sheared to keep them cool in hot weather, describe how wool is processed and how yarn is spun to weave warm clothing, blankets, and rugs. If your child does not know about sheep, show him a picture of a sheep and tell him how the sheep has wool instead of hair like we have. Describe how sheep are shorn in hot weather to keep them cool, like we have a haircut. Like a haircut, sheering does not hurt the sheep. This may be sufficient information for the day. At a later time, continue your presentation from where your story left off. End your story by saying, "Thank you for listening to my story. What would you like to do now?"

It is important to give your child adequate time to process any new information he receives. Wait until the following day to present additional information about wool. Over the course of a few weeks, you can use a map to show where sheep live in the world, tell simple stories about the history of wool, and read factual picture books about sheep, sheep herding, sheep dogs that help herd sheep, and wool processing. Sing songs about sheep such as "Mary Had a Little Lamb" and "Little Bo Peep." Take a day trip to visit a farm or petting zoo. Be creative with your related lessons and have fun!

Pattern Picture Cards

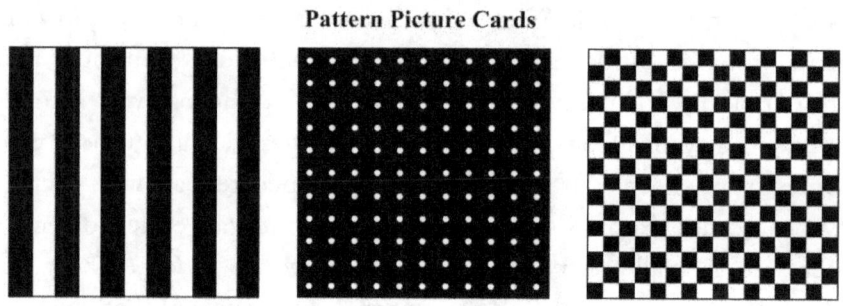

In addition to introducing fabric names, you can also introduce the names of patterns by making "Pattern Picture Cards." Picture Cards, which resemble flashcards, are a common way to introduce and reinforce vocabulary in the Montessori Primary classroom. To make Picture Cards, photocopy the pattern swatches in this book and mount each one on cardstock. Alternatively, you can print the patterns directly onto cardstock. Mount decorative paper from an art store on the reverse side of each Picture Card with spray glue outdoors in a well-ventilated area away from children, or use a glue stick. Make sure you use the same decorative paper on the back of each card in the set to promote a sense of classification. A less expensive alternative to decorative paper is paper from retired wallpaper books. Ask the owner of your local wallpaper store if there are any discontinued wallpaper books available for your child. Laminating the finished Picture Cards is optional. Keep in mind that coated papers, including some wallpapers, melt if laminated so do a sample test. Place up to ten Pattern Picture Cards in a deck at a time. Occasionally rotate Pattern Picture Cards to maintain interest.

Once you have created your Pattern Picture Cards, introduce contrasting pattern names three at a time using the Three Period Lesson technique: "Naming," "Recognition," and "Remembering." Isolate three Picture Cards on a table or rug. Point to each Picture Card in turn as you say their names: "This is 'hound's-tooth,'" "These are 'pinstripes,'" "These are 'polka dots.'" This concludes "Naming," the first period of the Three Period Lesson. Give commands such as, "Pick up the 'pinstripes,'" "Slide the 'hound's-tooth' here," or "Hand me the 'polka dots.'" Continue to give commands until your child is confident or loses interest. This concludes "Recognition," the second period of the Three Period Lesson. Point to each Pattern Picture Card one at a time saying, "What is this?" This concludes "Remembering," the third period of the Three Period Lesson. Depending on your child's level of confidence, accuracy, and interest, you can introduce three more pattern names or transition to the next activity. After your child has learned the names of multiple patterns, research their histories and geographic origins in order to create related activities.

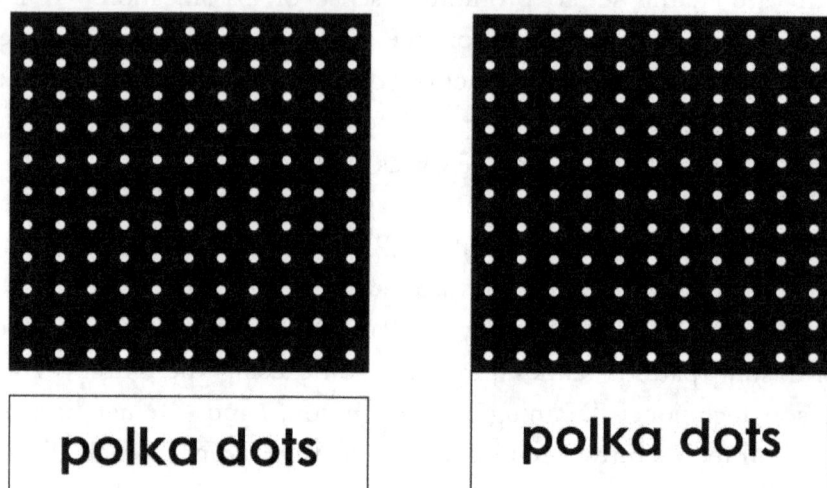

For literate children who know several fabric and pattern names, you can further expand their experiences with fabrics and patterns by creating "Three Part Cards." Three Part Cards, which are an extension of Picture Cards, are composed of three parts: unlabeled Picture Cards, Typed Labels, and labeled Picture Cards called "Control Cards." To make Three Part Cards for fabric names, glue a swatch of each previously introduced fabric onto cardstock. These swatches will act as the unlabeled Picture Cards. Make separate sans-serif, lower-case Typed Labels for each fabric card. Century Gothic typeface in 42 point font is recommended for captions. Glue or mount fabric swatches identical to those on the unlabeled Picture Cards onto correctly labeled cardstock. Be careful to not let glue bleed through the swatches which could alter the fabric texture.

Before using the Three Part Cards, review the corresponding Picture Card fabric swatches with your child. If your child is not confident with the Picture Cards, save the Three Part Cards for another day. When your child knows the Picture Cards, show him how the unlabeled Picture Cards in the Three Part Cards set are identical to the swatches in the Fabric Boxes. Organize the Three

Part Cards set of unlabeled Picture Cards face up on the far left-hand side of the work surface in a column with a small amount of space between each card. Show your child the Typed Labels next. Ask him to read the first Typed Label aloud to test for literacy. If the written vocabulary is too challenging, gracefully end the lesson by saying, "Let's look at this another day. What would you like to do now?" Put the cards away for another time and help your child transition to the next activity.

If your child can read with confidence and accuracy, place the stack of Typed Labels face up at the bottom center of the workspace. Pick up the first label in the stack. Tell your child you are going to put the label with the correct picture. Place the first Typed Label under its corresponding Picture Card. Allow your child to label the remaining Picture Cards. When your child is finished, introduce the Control Cards. Point out how these cards are labeled so your child can check his work. Place the Control Cards face up at the bottom center of the workspace. Pick up the first Control Card in the stack. Tell your child you are going to match it with the correct label. It is important to emphasize that the purpose of the Control Card is to match the words rather than the fabrics or pictures as Three Part Cards are designed as a literacy exercise rather than a picture matching activity. Allow your child to match the remaining Control Cards to their corresponding Typed Labels. Help him sort out any errors. Your child can now play this game independently. Rotate cards occasionally with new ones to maintain interest, strengthen vocabulary memory, and encourage reading.

To make Three Part Cards for patterns, mount each pattern on cardstock. These are the unlabeled Picture Cards. Create Typed Labels for pattern vocabulary such as "polka dots," "pinstripes," "hound's-tooth," "herringbone," "paisley," and "checks." Mount patterns identical to those used for the unlabeled Picture Cards onto correctly labeled cardstock. These are the Control Cards. Invite your child to use the Pattern Three Part Cards set the same way he used the Fabric Three Part Cards set.

In addition to making a Pattern Three Part Cards set, explore patterns with older children by looking at photographs of repeating geometric designs, fabric designs in fashions, examples of ancient architecture, tessellations, and the Fibonacci sequence in flower petals and other aspects of nature.

Be creative and have fun with fabrics and patterns together!

Other Titles in the
My First Montessori Book Series

My First Montessori Book of Colors

My First Montessori Book of Land and Water Forms

My First Montessori Book of Leaf Shapes

My First Montessori Book of Music Notation

My First Montessori Book of Shapes

My First Montessori Book of Telling Time

For a complete list of titles, visit the author's website at:

http://themontessorimysteryunveiled.weebly.com